Peregri
Completely Misleading
Guide to
SPORTS

Also in Beaver by Jim and Duncan Eldridge
How to Handle Grown-Ups
What Grown-Ups Say and What They Really Mean
Bogeys, Boils and Belly Buttons
More Ways to Handle Grown-Ups
Peregrine Peabody's Completely Misleading History of
the World
Bad Boyes
Bad Boyes and the Gangsters

Also by Jim Eldridge
The Wobbly Jelly Joke Book

Peregrine Peabody's Completely Misleading Guide to
SPORTS

Jim and Duncan Eldridge

Illustrated by David Mostyn

BEAVER BOOKS

A Beaver Book
Published by Arrow Books Limited
62–5 Chandos Place, London WC2N 4NW

An imprint of Century Hutchinson Ltd

London Melbourne Sydney Auckland
Johannesburg and agencies throughout the world

First published 1989

Text © Jim and Duncan Eldridge 1989
Illustrations © Century Hutchinson Ltd 1989

This book is sold subject to the condition that it shall
not, by way of trade or otherwise, be lent, resold,
hired out, or otherwise circulated without the
publisher's prior consent in any form of binding or
cover other than that in which it is published and
without a similar condition including this condition being imposed on the subsequent purchaser.

Set in Century Schoolbook
by JH Graphics Ltd, Reading

Printed and bound in Great Britain by
Courier International Ltd, Tiptree, Essex

ISBN 0 09 964580 7

Contents

Introduction

Hello, allow me to introduce myself. My name is Peregrine Peabody and I am a Genius. (I was going to say The Genius, but I am nothing if not modest.)

Following the astounding success of my first book, *Peregrine Peabody's Complete History of the World* (which, incidentally, they misprinted on the cover as *Peregrine Peabody's Completely Misleading History of the World,* the idiots!), my publisher Ms Beaver has asked me to put together a second book containing more of my Great Knowledge. So, here it is: *Peregrine Peabody's Complete Guide to Sports* (and let's hope they get the title right this time!).

Peregrine Peabody

Peregrine Peabody

PART ONE

Team Sports

Team sports are played by gangs of people who do not get on with each other but are all supposed to be on the same side. They are always shouting at each other, things like, 'You idiot! Fancy missing that!' and 'It's your fault we lost!'

Team sports are therefore to be avoided unless you don't mind fights and arguments.

Teams vary in size, from two to a million, depending on the particular sport being played. Personally I prefer a team of one, but then it becomes a Solo Sport, but 'So What!', that's what I say, and Yah Boo Sucks Poo to everyone who disagrees with me.

Cricket

This game is called 'cricket' because it began life as a contest in New Mexico between a family of crickets and a family of grasshoppers as to who was the most agile. The crickets were the Leg family, and the grasshoppers were the Stop family who lived over the road and had got fed up with the crickets leaping about all over the place and boasting how high they could jump. The Stop family challenged the Leg family to a game in which they would throw a peanut around, and the family that kept the peanut in the air the longest would be the winners.

The Leg family felt very confident but unfortunately the day before the contest the whole family got run over by a covered wagon. As a result when they turned up they were all badly damaged. The grasshoppers were delighted when they saw the injured crickets arrive, and they began to call them names, depending on what sort of injury they had suffered. 'Look,' they chortled, 'look at old Short Leg!' or, 'There's Square Leg!' and so on. The crickets said nothing, but just bobbled on to the field in a dignified manner.

'We'll win easily,' said Short Stop to his cousins, Long Stop, Full Stop and Bus Stop. 'Right, let's go!'

And with that the game got into full swing. Within minutes it was all over. As expected, the injured crickets dropped their peanut almost as soon as the game had started.

'Hoorah!' yelled the grasshoppers, and they all started jumping about and shouting and rubbing their back legs together noisily. This woke up a Sioux Indian called Fred who was asleep in his wigwam nearby. Fred staggered out of his wigwam, saw all these grasshoppers jumping up and down making a noise, trod on them, then went back to bed.

The crickets looked at the now flat grasshoppers lying about all over the place; then they looked at each other.

'As the other team have all just died,' said Long Leg, 'I think we can say we have won.'

This was the legend that was then passed on from hand to mouth through the Sioux nations, and became a tribal ritual acted out by the Sioux on Bank Holidays as they told the story in dance form of Winning Cricket, Short Stop, Square Leg, and all the others.

By the time Sir Walter Raleigh arrived in America this dance had become a proper game amongst the Indians, only they had added bits of their own, which included two Indians going into a cave and coming out with a bat each. No one could quite work out what the significance of this was, although the bats got pretty fed up with it. There they would be, hanging upside down and grabbing a quiet sleep, and next minute – grab! and they'd be part of the ritual.

Sir Walter Raleigh was fascinated by this game and he brought it back with him to England. So it was that 'cricket' became the National Game of England. (It is worth noting here that if the crickets had lost, today we would be playing a game called 'grasshopper' instead.)

The first thing the English did was to make the game completely incomprehensible to everyone, including those who played it. To do this they made up four new rules:

1 A batsman was In when he went Out. When he was Out he went In.

2 Every team would have eleven people on it. They would also have someone called The Twelfth Man, who did not exist. If he did exist then he would be known as The Third Man.

3 Only a man called Over is allowed to throw the ball at the bowler.

4 The batsman must have one long leg that goes all the way from his foot to the top of his head. (This is so that when the ball hits the batsman on the ear he can be called out 'leg before wicket'.)

In addition, to make the game very English, the people who threw the ball had to wear bowler hats, which is why they were called 'bowlers'.

Baseball

Baseball would be like an American version of cricket, if it wasn't for the fact that it is completely different.

What many people do not know is that baseball is actually a ritual re-enactment of the American War of Independence. A man symbolizing the Armies of King Zog walks into a big field armed only with a club. He stands in the middle of the field and shouts, 'I am the representative of Good King Zog of England, Scotland, Ireland, Wales and all points North of the Arctic Circle and I call upon you to pay homage!'

At this the twelve other people on the field, who represent the original American States, all start chucking rocks at the man with the club. The man with the club then has to try and hit the rocks before they hit him. As this is an almost impossible task he usually fails and so gets hit on the head with the rocks, ending up with a face like the White Cliffs of Dover. It is for this reason that most American heroes are called Rocky or Rock (e.g. Rocky Schicklegruber; Rock N. Roll; Rocky O'Grady Prune-Juice; Rock of Gibraltar).

Rugby Football

Rugby football is a game played only by idiots as it involves one person holding a ball, and then everybody on the field jumping on him and beating the daylights out of him.

WHERE'S EVERYONE?

At fixed times play stops so that most of the players can get in a big huddle in the middle of the field. This is so that they can get together to tell silly jokes and make nasty whispered comments about the spectators sitting watching them, such as (*nasty whispered comment*):

'See that man in the third row, hasn't he got a funny head!'

and (*silly joke*):

'My dog's got no nose.'
'Your dog's got no nose? How does he smell?'
'Terrible!'

It is worth pointing out that most of the people who play rugby are medical students. This is because it is a cheap way to get dead bodies to practise on. After every game the surviving medical students can usually be seen walking around the pitch stuffing those who didn't make it into sacks.

New Zealand has a very successful international rugby team. This is a result of their method of selecting players.

All the candidates line up on the pavement on one side of the main street in Wellington at rush hour. As soon as the traffic starts going really fast a selector waves a flag and all the candidates run across the road. Those who get to the other side are put into the New Zealand rugby team.

Australian Rules Football

Australian Rules Football is much like any other form of football, except it has only two rules. They are:

1 It begins.

2 It ends.

This means that anything is allowed. Consequently a person who plays Australian Rules Football is easily recognized because he is usually walking around encased in plaster or being pushed around in a wheelchair with his head under his arm. It is a very rough game indeed and you should not play it unless you are immune to being trampled by herds of wildebeest, being run over by tanks, or blown up by nuclear missiles.

Fortunately for the rest of the world Australian Rules Football is mainly played in Australia. If it was played in Scotland it would be known as Scotland Rules Football, which would give the Scots delusions of grandeur about being the best footballing nation in the world.

American Football

'American Football' is a completely misleading name because:

1 No player ever touches the ball with their foot; and

2 It isn't played by Americans at all but by aliens from other planets such as Mars, Pluto and Donald Duck.

These aliens are so huge and so horrible to look at that they have to be completely encased in enormous suits of plastic with masks over their faces. No one has ever seen an American Football player without this covering on. It is said that if you do your feet will go green and you will be turned to stone.

All these aliens are androids who have to be wound up with an enormous key before the start of every game. Once they are wound up they are sent out on the field, where they lumber around and crash into each other until their mechanism runs down and they fall over.

Football (Soccer)

Football is the greatest game in the world, and Wigthorpe Wanderers United are the greatest football team in the world. There is nothing more you need to know about football. Once you have these two facts at your fingertips you know everything of real importance about the game. However, for those of you who are determined to fill your heads with useless and unimportant facts, here is a fascinating story from the History of Football.

It was 1924 and it was the final of the Animal World Cup. The match was between Koala Rovers of Australia and Insects and Vermin United of England, and Insects and Vermin were struggling. They were already seven goals to nil down halfway through the second half, and their centre-forward, Martin Millipede, still hadn't appeared on the pitch. Even as the crowd watched, Koala Rovers slammed their eighth goal into the back of Insects and Vermin's net. The situation looked hopeless for Insects and Vermin.

And then out on to the pitch ran Martin Millipede, his thousand legs waving in the strong sunlight.

'Millipede! Millipede!' roared the crowd.

Straight from the kick-off Ronnie Rodent slipped the ball to Martin Millipede. The Insects' centre-forward hurtled through Koala Rovers' defence and slammed the ball into their net past the helpless keeper. 8-1.

From then on the game belonged to Insects and Vermin. When the final whistle went the score was 10-8 to Insects and Vermin, and every one of the I and V goals had been scored by Martin Millipede.

As the two teams left the pitch, Curly Koala turned to the I and V captain, Ronnie Rodent, a look of astonishment on his face.

'Unbelievable!' he said. 'Ten goals in fifteen minutes! What a player!'

'He certainly is,' agreed Ronnie Rodent.

'There's one thing I still don't understand, though,' said Curly.

'What's that?' asked Ronnie.

'Why did you wait until halfway through the second half to bring him on. If he'd come on at the start you'd have slaughtered us.'

'I know,' said Ronnie with a sigh. 'The trouble is it takes him so long to do his boots up.'

Gaelic Football

As with many sports and games, this title is the result of a mis-spelling. It was originally called *Garlic* Football. Why? Well, a team called Dunstable Warriors were so fed up with losing all their games that they hit on an astounding new tactic. The whole team took to eating huge quantities of garlic, and whenever the other team got the ball they breathed on them. This caused the players from the other team to fall unconscious.

Dunstable Warriors' centre-forward would then take possession of the ball, rush up to the opposing goalkeeper, breathe on him, and score as soon as he'd fallen over.

Rounders

Rounders is a similar sport to Angling (See *Angling* page 64), except that where Angling is concerned with Angles (the crooked bits in straight lines, corners of triangles, etc.), Rounders is concerned with things that are round (e.g. circles and balls and such).

The object of the game is for each team to find as many round things as possible in a certain space of time. The team with the most round things when the final whistle blows is the winner.

Examples of round things are:

A Round Tuit This will mend or solve everything in the whole world, as can be seen from the fact that when you ask someone if they've mended their bike, tidied their room, or put the cat out on Venus, they always answer: 'I'll do it when I get a Round Tuit.'

A Round of Sandwiches This means a whole sandwich cut into bits so that it makes it easier to eat. I think this is wrong, I find a sandwich easier to eat if it is left completely whole and just crammed inside the mouth in one go. After all, this system works for pythons, why shouldn't it work for humans?

Hanging A-Round This means lounging inside a circle with a round thing dangling on a bit of string. If the thing goes up and down the string then it's a Yo-Yo and isn't counted.

Netball is similar to fishing, except instead of using a rod and line you use a long pole with a net at the end. The object of this sport is to get your ball out of a pond after some rotten bully has kicked it in. However, it is important that you do not do this unless an adult is around, in case you fall in. In fact, get the adult to do it for you instead. If they fall in it doesn't matter so much.

Basketball

This is a game where very tall thin people (who bang their heads on the ceiling when they walk into an ordinary room) throw a ball at one another and drop it from a great height into a basket screwed to a wall. Because it is a game designed for giants no one is allowed to play if they are under three metres tall. All short people (i.e. those under three metres tall) who wish to become basketball players have to undergo a severe form of training called Grow-Quick.

They are planted by their feet into a large flower pot, and fertilizer and water are poured on to the earth. After five days the trainer (usually a Head Gardener at a local Garden Centre) goes to check how well they are growing. It is at this point that all unlikely prospects are weeded out. These include:

1   Those people who have not grown one little bit.

2   Those people who have shrunk due to their feet being stuck in damp earth.

3   Those people who have begun to sprout flowers and/or branches or other green leafy bits.

The ones who are left then spend another week or so in their flower pots. By this time they have either grown that extra bit to push them over three metres, or they have turned into trees or bushes.

The successful three-metre-achievers are given a certificate telling them they are now fully authorized basketball players and can walk about, bashing their heads against ceilings and frightening the general public by towering over them. The trees or bushes are sold at a handsome profit to the Garden Centre owners.

Hockey

Hockey is an exceedingly dangerous game which consists of two teams of people rushing around a field pretending to hit a ball with long wooden sticks, but in reality bashing each other. For this reason it is a game to be avoided at all costs.

Hockey first made its appearance in the twelfth century, as a way of getting rid of caterpillars from people's vegetable gardens. In 1137 there was a plague of caterpillars in the village of Hockey-in-the-Mud, and it looked as if the whole lettuce crop would be wiped out. People had tried everything, but the caterpillars just kept appearing every morning in large numbers and eating all the lettuces.

A parish meeting was held, and one villager, George Ball, said there was only one thing to do — attack the caterpillars physically as they ate. So the villagers went out in the middle of the night and sawed branches off the trees. Then, next morning, as the caterpillars came out of hiding and started eating the lettuces, the villagers attacked. They leapt upon the lettuce patch and started laying about them left and right. Sure enough the caterpillars got so frightened that they all leapt off the lettuces and rushed off to the next village.

The villagers danced about with delight. Or, at least, they did until one of them noticed that, because of all this bashing with branches and dancing, every single lettuce had been flattened. The villagers were so mad that they all started to chase around looking for George Ball. They bashed haystacks and bushes trying to flush him out. But George had realized what was happening, and had tactfully decided to seek his fortune in London right away.

However, that is why the game of rushing around waving long bent bits of wood and bashing a ball with them is named after the village where it all started, Hockey (in-the-Mud).

This is the same as Hockey, except it is played while eating ice cream.

SCRUNCH!
SCRUNCH!

Polo

This, of course, was the game invented by the Irish explorer, Mark O'Polo, inventor of the mint of the same name. Very little more needs to be said about this game except that it involves horses and mallets and chukkas. The chukkas are the people who chuck the horses back on the field if they run off after being frightened by all these people with mallets.

Lacrosse

This is the French version of Noughts and Crosses (Le Noughte et La Crosse) but as it is played only with Crosses it is called Lacrosse.

Tug of War

Tug of War is like Man of War, only different. A Man of War is a kind of jellyfish thing and is very dangerous; Tug of War is equally dangerous, and also involves jellyfish things.

Tug of War consists of two teams being tied together; and then someone throws a dangerous kind of jellyfish thing between them and they have to run away from it as fast as they can. This is a very cruel sport and the Society for Protection Against Cruelty to Kinds of Jellyfish Things (SPACKJET) have, quite rightly, organized a nation-wide petition and lobbied their MPs with a view to banning it.

Because of this cruel sport, kinds of jellyfish things have become endangered species and the organizers of this 'sport' have had great difficulty in finding enough to continue. They have therefore had to resort to using other objects in place of the jellyfish things, e.g. planks of wood, old boots, nuclear weapons, earthquakes, etc. These are a bit more dangerous for the humans involved, but a lot safer for the poor old kinds of jellyfish things.

PART TWO

Athletics

Athletics are sports usually carried out by people wearing only their vest and underpants. This proves that Athletics is one of the truly 'early' sports, as those are the kind of clothes you wear when you get up early and before you have put on the rest of your clothes.

Why this is all the clothing that athletes wear is one of the Great Mysteries of the Universe, along with:

Who built the Pyramids? (For the answer to this see *Peregrine Peabody's Complete History of the World.*)

Why does toast always fall on the buttered side when you drop it?

and

Where do all the pencils go when you want one?

Running

This is easily done by everybody who owns two feet, preferably each of them on a separate leg. However, in Professional Athletics it is made harder because the athletes have to run over a track made out of old gas and electricity meters. Some of these tracks are only a hundred meters long, but some are ten thousand meters long, which means there is a lot more chance of runners getting their feet caught in one of the little clocks that go round to tell you how much gas or electricity you've used.

Hurdles

This is the same as running over gas and electricity meters with the additional obstacle of having a five-barred farm gate every ten meters or so. The reason this particular race developed was because the runners who lived in the country claimed that the runners who lived in towns and cities had an unfair advantage over them because of all the practice that they got running for buses.

'We don't have any buses in the country,' they complained.

'Well what do you have?' asked the Athletics Organizers.

The country runners thought for a minute.

'Cows,' they said, 'and farm gates.'

'Right,' said the Athletics Organizers, and they brought in a load of cows and farm gates to try and make the race a little fairer. However the cows all disappeared halfway through the first race for a quiet munch of some grass. The farm gates, not having legs, had to stay where they were, and that is how Hurdles came about.

The Marathon

'Marathon' is a Greek word which means, 'Who can tell Doctor Doctor jokes for the longest time without stopping for breath or using a full stop'. The World Record was created in 1988 at the London Marathon (a massive event where 100 000 people assembled and all told Doctor Doctor jokes at once), by Daisy FizNoodle of Westphalia. Her marathon run went like this:

'Doctor doctor I think I'm a yo-yo! Sit down sit down sit down sit down; Doctor doctor I feel like a pack of cards! I'll deal with you later; Doctor doctor I keep thinking I'm a pair of curtains! Pull yourself together; Doctor doctor I keep thinking I'm two people! Could you repeat that and this time don't both speak at once; Doctor doctor I can't sleep! Lie on the edge of the bed and you'll soon drop off; Doctor doctor I think I'm a bird! I'll tweet you in a minute. Doctor doctor I snore so loudly I keep myself awake! Sleep in another room.'

High Jump

The High Jump means seeing who can jump the highest, and the best jumper who ever lived was Norman Normal of Sydney, Australia, who, while preparing to go to the toilet out in the bush accidentally sat on a porcupine.

Low Jump

This differs from the High Jump in that the jumper has to do absolutely nothing at all except fall over. The distance between their highest point (i.e. the back of their head if they have fallen face down) and the ground is then measured, and the one with the smallest measurement wins. The World Record for the Low Jump is held by Ivan Flatfoot of Perth, who, while lying down waiting to be measured, was accidentally run over by a steamroller and completely flattened.

Long Jump

Most people think that the way to achieve the best ever Long Jump is by running a long way, hurling yourself forward through the air as far as you can, and then landing in some soft sand. Wrong! It must be obvious to everyone that the running bit is going to use up all your energy, so you are not going to do a really good jump. The answer, therefore, is to use the Peregrine Peabody Long Jump Machine.

This consists of a giant rubber band stretched between two bits of wood at the start of the Long Jump sandpit. What you do is stand leaning back against the taut rubber band, and then you run *away* from the sandpit. You will not have to run far, because the rubber band will stretch just a little bit more before it goes Twang!

At this point you will find your feet leaving the ground and your body hurtling through the air.

It is important at this point that you make sure that you achieve a proper landing in the soft sand. At my first attempt using this method I landed upside down. This disqualifies you in competition as the judges expect you to land on your feet. Personally I consider this unfair and discrimination, at least until I get my Long Jump Machine perfected. The only problem with using my Machine is I have not yet worked out how to get the sand out of my nose after each jump.

Short Jump

This is similar to the Low Jump, except that the jumper does not even have to fall over. All the jumper has to do is stand nice and still until the distance he or she has not jumped is measured.

Interest in this particular athletic event waned when it was discovered that everybody in the entire universe held the World Record of Zero point Zero Zero Zero centimetres.

Putting the Shot

This is another name for Hide and Seek. Each competitor is given a large ball of iron and has to go and put it somewhere in the stadium. Then all the spectators have to look for it. The winner is the one who finds it.

A very ancient sport, whose name is actually a mis-spelling of 'discuss'. In this event all the competitors talk about things amongst themselves. The aim is to find the Most Boring Talker in the World. One by one the competitors fall asleep as they discuss things, until in the end only one Discusser is left awake, and that is The Winner.

Practising for this event in every country is usually done in that country's Houses of Parliament or Senate.

Throwing the Hammer

The World Record for Throwing the Hammer is held by a carpenter from Scotland, Angus McBain of Kinlochspelve on the Isle of Mull.

Angus was banging nails into a roof he was building for his house, when his neighbour Jamie McBruin came past.

'Good morning, Angus!' said Jamie.

'Hmph!' grunted back Angus, who was not known for his good humour.

'I heard a joke this morning on the radio and straight away I thought of you,' said Jamie.

'Hmph,' grunted Angus again.

'Yes,' Jamie continued. 'How do you keep an idiot in suspense?'

'I dinnae know,' said Angus. 'How?'

With that Jamie laughed, and then walked off. Angus stopped work and rested on his ladder, watching Jamie disappear down the road and wondering what the point of the joke was. It was a full fifteen minutes before Angus realized.

'You insulting idiot!' he yelled, and he hurled the hammer he was holding at the distant figure of Jamie. The hammer hit Jamie on the head and killed him.

When the police measured the distance between Angus's roof and Jamie's body for evidence they found it was almost a mile. The result was Angus received fifteen years in jail for murder, and also a medal as the new World Record Holder for Throwing the Hammer.

Javelin and Pole Vault Combined

Javelin and Pole Vault are not usually thought of as one event, but in the 1976 Olympics two most bizarre incidents occurred which linked them together.

The competitor from Iceland in the Decathlon, one Finn O'Gnasher, had had a rough evening the night before his event, mainly due to a terrifying plane journey from

Iceland to wherever it was the Olympics were being held that year. He was down to take part in two events that morning: the Javelin and the Pole Vault. Unfortunately Finn was so disoriented by jet-lag and a bad case of tummy upset after a terrible meal on the plane that he got into a state of confusion. Such was his confusion that when they gave him the long pole for the pole vault, he ran with it towards the high bar, tripped, and the pole flew out of his hand and sailed across the arena, where it stuck in the grass and won Finn the Gold Medal in the javelin event.

The other competitors in the javelin event were furious and complained to the judges. In an effort to calm the situation the judges ordered Finn to pick up the javelin and throw it, just to see if he could achieve the same record throw. This time Finn picked up the javelin, ran with it, but unfortunately his hands were so sweaty that the javelin stuck to his palms. This time, therefore, when he hurled the javelin it thudded point down into the ground by his feet. Finn O'Gnasher was lifted off the ground by the force of it, and promptly sailed over the high bar of the Pole Vault, creating a new World Record in that event.

At this the other competitors and the crowd went mad. Faced with the possibility of a riot, the judges there and then made up a new event: Javelin and Pole Vault Combined, and made Finn O'Gnasher the only ever World Champion and Olympic Record Holder.

Decathlon

The Decathlon is an amazing athletic event because it involves doing a whole lot of different athletic activities. These include:

Pushing a peanut up a mountain with your nose.

Making squeaky noises with your armpit.

Balancing on your head in a bucket of raspberry jelly.

Making an electric drill out of a woodpecker, a washing up liquid bottle and a 2volt battery.

Having a bath without losing the soap.

Removing your own appendix using only a teaspoon and two elastic bands.

Stuffing a duvet with your own belly button fluff.

Translating the Birmingham Phone Book into Chinese.

So far there has only ever been one winner of this event: Albert Einstein, who managed it all by discovering Relativity, which meant that he got 10 trillion points all in one go for being a Clever Clogs.

Relay Races

Relay Races are really odd races. They are like three-legged races except that in relay races there are *four* runners who all have their legs tied together. This means eight legs, all but two tied up, and to date no one has ever even started in a relay race, let alone finished. This is because by the time the four runners have worked out how even to move, the whistle has gone for the end of the race.

This is quite easily done. Put down one foot. Put the other foot in front of the first. Lift up the first foot you put down, and then place that foot in front of the second foot. Then move that second foot (which has now become the first foot) and place that in front of the first foot (which has now become the second foot). If a third foot should appear while you are engaged in this sport then you have an unfair advantage and will be disqualified.

Five-Legged Race

The Five-Legged Race is a race for people with five legs, and the only ever World Champion and Olympic Record Holder was Ivor Twentyffetoes. As his name suggests, he did in fact have five legs and he is the only genuine contestant ever recorded. Others have tried to enter for this race but all of them were found to be fakes in some way. These fake entrants included an octopus who hid three of its legs under a wig; an elephant who tied a shoe on to the end of its trunk; and three men (one of whom only had one leg) who were hiding inside the same large suit as part of a plan to escape from prison.

Pancake Race

The Pancake Race is put in School Sports especially so that parents can show off that they can

1 Cook a Pancake; and
2 Run while tossing it up and down in a frying pan.

In fact this race is a bit of a cheat because the *worst* pancake maker is nearly always the winner. This is because their pancakes are usually burnt and stuck to the frying pan. This means that they wouldn't fall out even if the contestant ran with the fying pan *upside down*.

In my opinion the only way to test the winner of a pancake race is for a judge (e.g. me) to eat the pancakes and so judge the winner. However, this would have to be done *before* the race in case an entrant dropped their pancake on the ground and it fell on something yukky and horrible, or accidentally got trodden on, in which case I wouldn't fancy putting it in *my* mouth and chewing it!

Sack Race

This is a most unusual event. The competitors line up at the starting tape; the whistle blows, and these huge people rush out of hiding, grab the competitors, stuff them inside sacks and then tie the tops up.

The competitors then shout and holler like mad and demand to be let out, while the huge people rush off and put everyone else they can find into sacks. What it's all about is a complete mystery to most sporting experts. My own personal theory, based on a study of pre-historic writing, is that it is an ancient ritual designed to stop people from getting sun-burned. However, this action has become unnecessary since the invention of sun-tan cream.

Egg and Spoon Race

The Egg and Spoon Race is one of the greatest athletic events of all time. I can proudly say this because, as the St Barnabas Nursery School Junior Under-Six-Year-Old Egg and Spoon Champion, I can speak from experience. The trick is to fry your egg first. This makes sure it stays in the bowl of the spoon and doesn't roll off, as is usually the case with boiled eggs. In my case, as I was only five years old at the time of my Greatest Athletic Triumph, I had not yet learnt how to fry an egg, and was forced by the organizer of this event (a certain Miss Purves) to use the ordinary common or garden oval shaped hard-boiled egg. The result was that it kept rolling off my spoon.

I solved this problem by wrapping sticky tape round the egg and spoon so they were fixed securely together. It was by this brilliant method that I won my Great Race.

Unfortunately for me the other children complained and I was disqualified when Miss Purves discovered the sticky tape holding my hard-boiled egg to the spoon. The bag of boiled sweets I had won was rudely taken away from me and given to a horrible little girl called Samantha Breadbasket.

However, as far as I am concerned, I was awarded First Price and so can claim it as a Great Victory.

PART THREE

Solo Sports
(Individual Skill Sports)

Solo Sports are so called because they are not
very high on the list of sports. In fact they are
pretty low down on that list, so low, in fact,
that that is how they got their name ('So-lo').

Solo sports are also known as 'individual
skill sports'. The word 'individual' comes from
an old Cherokee Indian word meaning, 'Man
who walks on one leg and falls over and is left
all alone in the middle of the desert because
his knees smell'. Therefore an Individual Skill
Sport is one that is played by one person on
their own. This means that, as that person is
the only one playing, they usually come first
and win. (However, this is not always the
case. I once played a game of draughts with
myself and lost 3 games to 1. But then that's
the sort of thing that can only happen to a
Genius like me.)

Tennis

Not many people know that originally this game was called 'Sixnish' because it was played by six people at a time, until one day another four people turned up with rackets wanting to have a game, which led to the name being changed to Tennish. The 'h' was dropped because a signwriter who was painting the sign for the very first Wimbledon Tennish Tournament ran out of space at the end of the board.

Tennis has a most unusual scoring system based on Romance and Drinking. Every time someone scores a point the Referee calls out 'Love!', and if the players score the same number of points the referee calls out 'Juice!'

The greatest Tennis players of all time include:

Pedro da Crunch, who was born with eight arms, which gave him a great advantage. He even won the Wimbledon Mixed Doubles Championship on his own.

Dxscv Zxcvhchvzcs, a brilliant Rumanian women's champion who won without anyone ever knowing who she was because none of the commentators could pronounce her surname.

Hector Nutter, a famous American player who was useless at tennis but became famous for losing his temper. The reason he lost his

temper was because he couldn't play properly.
Instead he used to walk on court and get angry
and jump up and down on his opponent's
tennis racket. This meant they had nothing to
play with so Nutter was declared the winner.
In this way he won five Wimbledon Championships in a row without once hitting a ball.

Boris Bucket, the famous banjo player who
became a tennis star by accident when he
turned up at the wrong place to give a concert
of banjo music. He thought the people hitting
balls at him were doing it as a way of making
nasty comments about his banjo playing, so he
used his banjo to knock the balls back at them.
He was noticeable as the only player ever to
win two World Championships using a banjo
as a tennis racket. His career came to an
untimely end when the G string on his banjo
broke.

Little Nelly Peabody, my aunt, and the
Greatest Women's Tennis Player of All Time.
Unfortunately she was never allowed to play
at Wimbledon (or anywhere else in public)
because she suffered from halitosis of the feet,
a condition which knocked out everyone standing within ten metres of her. However, if she
had been allowed to play she would have been
World Champion for Ever.

Table Tennis

Table Tennis is similar to ordinary Tennis, except that it is played on a table. Unfortunately, many players have sustained serious injuries when they fall off the table as they chase after a difficult shot. Other injuries include:

players leaping over the net to congratulate the winner of the game and knocking themselves out as they bash their heads on the ceiling;

strained knee muscles when players first climb on to the table;

bruises resulting from treading on knives and forks and other cutlery that may have been left on the table by the last people to use it.

Because of all of these the International Sports Association are considering banning Table Tennis as one of the most dangerous of all sports.

Squash

This is the name given to a sport where the object is to get as many people into a railway carriage as possible. It is played every morning and late afternoon on weekdays in every major capital across the world.

Badminton

Like many games, this one is now known by an incorrect name. When it was first invented by Maori Chief Nurgle Minton of New Zealand in 1147 it was called *Goodminton*.

The game consisted of chucking a load of feathers up into the air and trying to head them towards goal. However, people who tried it soon complained that it was impossible, because the feathers just kept fluttering down. Soon all Goodminton players were convinced that they were failures as athletes, so they all got very depressed. Two years after the game was first played the whole Maori population of New Zealand was walking around in a state of depression. Eventually a Maori doctor worked out that there must be a link between the game of Goodminton and this general depression. As a result all the Maoris started grumbling about the game, which is how it came to be called *Badminton*.

This change of name greatly upset Chief Nurgle Minton because he took all the moaning as a slur on his name (which it was). In a great huff he decided to give up being king. He handed over his throne to his son, Wobble Minton. Fortunately for the Maoris, Wobble Minton was more intelligent than his father and he realized why the feathers were so hard to head successfully. To solve the problem he designed a lump of cork, which the feathers were stuck into.

As a result, every Maori was able to head the feathers straight into goal. However, this did not please everybody. Because it became so easy to score goals, the games began to have results like 100-98. This upset the scorers (who had to do a lot of work keeping count of all the goals), and also the goalkeepers, who walked around very depressed because so many goals were getting past them.

The goalkeepers got so fed up that they invented a bat to bash the corked feathers with whenever they came near them. This bat made such a loud noise when it hit the cork that the other players complained, 'We can't hear with that racket!' which is how the badminton bat got its name.

Bowls

These are things you eat soup and breakfast cereals out of, and why anyone should think they have anything to do with sport is beyond me. However the publisher, Ms Beaver, gave me this list of sports, and on it was this word 'bowls'. I can only assume that she is an idiot, or she gave me her shopping list by mistake and now she will go out shopping and forget to buy any bowls for her kitchen.

Cycling

The Tour de France

The Tour de France is so called because it is a bicycle race that takes place up and down the Tower ('tour' is French for tower) of France. As everyone knows, the Tower of France is the Eiffel Tower in Paris, a huge pointed construction that looks like a big radio mast.

Originally this race was going to be held in Italy, in which case it would have been known as the Tour de Italy. However, as the Tower (or 'tour') of Italy is the Tower of Pisa, and this tower leans at a dangerous angle, it was felt that many of the cyclists taking part in such a race might have fallen off at the bendy bit in the middle and been badly damaged by dropping to the ground some thirty metres below.

The way the race works is this: every year a few hundred cyclists from all over the world gather together at the bottom of the Eiffel Tower. They all ride different sorts of bikes: racing bikes, old-fashioned sit-up-and-beg bikes, penny-farthings, BMX bikes, mountain bikes, etc. Providing it looks like a bike and the power that drives it comes from the person sitting on it, then it qualifies as a bike.

They had to include this rule about 'the person sitting on it' because in 1957 someone turned up with a two-wheeled cart pulled by a horse, claiming that it was a bike because it had two wheels and it didn't have an engine.

There was a lot of argument about whether or not this really was a bike. In the end the organizers agreed to let the horse-drawn two-wheeled cart take part, and halfway up the Tower the horse got stuck and blocked the Tower for the next two days, causing the rest of the race to be cancelled. As a result, a tough new rule was introduced, to make sure the power was provided by 'the person on the bike'. This is a rule still being argued about by the Tandem Riders' Association, who claim that it prevents them taking part, even though their machines are bicycles, because the power is provided by two people.

In 1968 one pair of tandem riders found a way to get round this rule: the day before the race one of them had both his legs amputated. The organizers were therefore forced to let them enter the race, but they came last due to the extra weight on the machine, and no one has taken such drastic measures to get round this rule since.

Anyway, all the cyclists gather on their bikes at the foot of the stairs at the bottom of the Eiffel Tower. When everyone is ready a gen-darme blows his whistle and they start to pedal like mad and race their bikes up the stairs. Anyone found using the lifts is auto-matically disqualified.

When they get to the top of the Eiffel Tower they have to sign their name on the wall of the toilet to prove they have actually reached the top, before they cycle down. This business of signing one's name on the toilet wall requires great skill, and many would-be Tour de France competitors can be seen practising for the event in toilets and subways all over the world.

The 'signing your name' element is a relatively recent introduction to the race. Until 1974 the proof that a rider had got to the top was for him or her to be photographed there. However this practice was discontinued after a certain Emile Blanc won the race three times in a row, (1971–3). The organizers were at first impressed, but they got suspicious in 1973 when they noticed that Emile didn't appear to be even a little out of breath when he appeared at the bottom of the Eiffel Tower at the end of the race, and that his bike was still wrapped in cardboard. Further investigations showed that Emile Blanc was actually one of a pair of twins, and it was his twin who had been photographed at the top of the Tower, while Emile never even left the bottom. The puzzling thing was how Emile and his twin had got away with this con-trick for the previous two years, as his twin was in fact a girl, Charlotte Blanc, and the pair weren't even idential twins.

Finally, did you know that the Eiffel Tower is so called because when you arrive at the very top you get an amazing eye-full of a view of Paris? Well you know now.

Golf

Golf is a really bizarre game with a list of scoring terms and rules that make even cricket seem comprehensible. For example: it has a tee that you can't drink; it has a birdie that doesn't fly; and it has a scratch without an itch.

According to a book of rules I was given, the way to play golf is as follows:

First, you have to address the ball. (See what I mean? You have to stand there and say things like, 'Hello, ball,' or write your address on it, for no good reason at all!)

Having addressed the ball you pick up your golf club and shout 'Four!'. (This despite the fact that you only have *one* golf club in your hand, and you are only hitting *one* ball. If you had four golf clubs, or were about to hit four balls, it would make sense.) You then hit the ball, if you are lucky. If you are not, as happened to a friend of mine when he was playing golf for the first time, you hit the earth all around the ball and dig a deep hole into which you fall. This is known as One in a Hole, which is different from a Hole in One.

The ball will now sail through the air, hit various people on the head, bounce off a tree and fall into a huge piece of forest that hasn't been cleared for twenty years. You will go into this forest and start looking for your ball. While there you will find: *(a)* three explorers who have been lost in this wilderness for ten years; *(b)* a bunch of run-away convicts; *(c)* King Arthur and the Holy Grail; *(d)* King Kong.

You will hit your ball out of the forest, where it will roll down a sand dune and sink fifteen metres below ground level in sand. After hiring a JCB you will dig it out and hit it again. This time it will go into a lake that only deep sea divers and Loch Ness monsters have ever seen the bottom of. You will drain this lake and manage to hit your ball out of the sludge, and this time it will roll on to a large green patch of grass.

You will then attempt to hit your ball about a hundred times before you actually manage to get your club to knock against it. This time the ball will bounce along the grass and then drop into a small hole. This means you will have scored. Your score will either be a Par, a Birdie, an Eagle, an Albatross, a Bush, a Jam-pot, an Elephant, or a Five-Nosed Wombat with Bad Feet.

After this, thinking you have finished, you will go to get your tee from your caddy (which is where the name Tee-Caddy comes from). He will tell you you have to do all this another seventeen times before you have finished. This will make you so angry that you jump up and down on your golf clubs, breaking them and spraining your ankle. At which point you give up Golf and go off to find another sport to play.

Angling

Angling, as everyone knows, was first practised by that Ancient Saxon tribe, the Angles. It is a game that consist of throwing angles of different shapes and sizes at your opponent (e.g. a 90 degree angle, a 35 degree angle).

The object of the game is to catch as many angles as you can and then to reassemble them into a well-known shape (e.g. a triangle or a square).

Any player attempting to put them into a less-well-known shape (e.g. a rhombus or a squiggle) has all his or her angles straightened out and is automatically disqualified.

Archery

This is not really a sport at all but a hobby. It consists of listening to the BBC Radio serial *The Archers* so frequently that your ears go all curly and eventually drop off.

Ice-skating

Ice-skating is either very easy or very difficult, depending upon the type of ice you skate on.

If you skate on a wafer or a choc ice it is quite simple because both of these are generally flat-tish in shape. However, skating on a cornet is very difficult because it has a steep slope from the top of the cone wafer to the top of the ice itself.

If you skate on an ice cream cone that also has cherries and nuts on then the whole thing becomes impossible – only World Champions can achieve this.

Roller-skating

This is similar to ice-skating except that you do it on a roll (e.g. a cheese roll, a salad roll).

The most famous roller-skater of all time was Hilda Blewitt of Bognor. What not many people know is that Hilda was also a highly sucessful author and in her lifetime she published over one hundred books. The reason that not many people know this is because she always wrote under a nom-de-plume (the name of her pen) as she was very shy. Some of her best known books (and the names she wrote them under) were:

Measuring in Little Bits by Milly Metre
Late For School by Miss D. Bus
The Fitted Carpet by Walter Wall
The Hungry Dog by Norah Bone
Crime Doesn't Pay by Robin Banks
Punctured! by Buster Tire
A Light Snack by Roland Butter
The Broken Window by Eva Brick

Ski-ing

Ski-ing is a truly bizarre sport. Skiers allow themselves to be dumped on the top of a mountain with a couple of planks of wood tied to their feet, and then hurtle towards the bottom at enormous speed. It is therefore a sport for brainless idiots.

What many people do not know is how skiing originated. It happened in this way:

One day in 1672 a postman in Switzerland called Mynd Mifoot had a puncture in the front wheel of his bicycle. This meant that he was late for work on his postal round. In an attempt to let his village know that their post would be late he dragged his punctured bicycle up to the top of a nearby snow-capped mountain. His intention was to give a big shout from the top of the mountain, but first he set to work on his bike.

Twenty minutes later the puncture was fixed and Mynd Mifoot sat astride his bike, his feet on the pedals, his sack of mail around his neck, and called out, 'Yi yam a bit yolateeeeee!' In this way he invented the yodel.

Unfortunately for Mynd this shouting dislodged a large lump of snow at the top of the mountain, starting an avalanche which hurtled down and smacked him on the back of the neck.

'Aaaaarghhhh!!!!' went Mynd, and hurtled forward off his bike. It was even more unfortunate for him that he had just strapped his feet on to his pedals. As he shot forward the pedals snapped off his bike, and Mynd slid all the way down the mountainside on the pedals, his sack of mail still hanging round his neck. Which is how Mynd Mifoot became, not only the first person to invent both yodelling and ski-ing simultaneously, but also the fastest postman in history.

Show Jumping

'Show Jumping' is yet another wrong name given to a sport due to mis-spelling. The original name was *Shoe* Jumping, an ancient traditional event in which people put on shoes of the wrong sizes and jumped in them. (It was invented by a man called Jim Karna of Stoke Poges in 1143. Due to yet another mis-spelling, Jim's name has come down to us through history as Gymkhana, which is why Show Jumping events are called . . . you've guessed it.)

Anyway, to get back to shoe jumping: the rules of the event were that all the competitors went into a field, took off their shoes and put them in a big barrel. The barrel was given a good shake before the competitors reached into it, pulled out any two shoes and put them on. They then had to jump up and down in them for as long as they could. The one who kept jumping the longest was the winner.

The way that horses became included in the sport was as follows. In 1146 at the Fourth Annual Shoe Jumping Competition at Jim Karna's field, a large man called Fred the Blogg, who had size fifteen feet, drew two shoes out of the barrel, one a size Two and one a size Three. Both were left shoes.

Fred was upset because he had won the event for the past two years running (or jumping) and was determined to make it a hat-trick that year. With the aid of a crowbar and a pair of shears Fred was able to get the shoes on to his feet, but he wasn't able to walk into the centre of the field and start jumping. Determined not to be beaten he called for his horse, Whinny (so called because that was the only word she could say), climbed on her, and Whinny took him to the centre of the field.

Once at the centre of the field Fred was about to climb down off Whinny's back, when he found he'd got his braces tangled up with the saddle, so he couldn't get off.

'Oh well,' he thought, 'I'm still wearing the shoes, and I am in the field, so all I have to do is jump up and down on Whinny's back and I'll be all right.'

So, when Jim Karna gave the signal for everyone to start jumping, Fred began to jump up and down on his horse's back. Whinny was amazed by this and not a little indignant, and she started jumping up and down as well to give Fred a taste of his own medicine. Round and round the field she went, with Fred hanging grimly on to her bridle. The other Shoe Jumpers were astonished at this, and they all stopped to watch as Whinny went round and round again, with Fred bouncing up and down, until he finally fell off.

'The winner!' cried the bruised and battered Fred delightedly as Whinny trod on him.

All the other Shoe Jumpers then went off home in a sulk (or lots of sulks), claiming that Fred had won by cheating. So the next year, 1147, everyone turned up with a horse. And since that day Shoe (or Show) Jumping has always been performed on horses.

Darts

The greatest darts player of all was Sir Robin Loxley, a.k.a. Robin Hood.

One evening Robin Hood was in the Old Duck and Ferret in the middle of Sherwood Forest, drinking a pint of goodly ale with his Merrie Men (they were Merrie because they had been drinking ale since nine o'clock that morning) when in walked a cloaked stranger.

'I hear,' saith this cloaked stranger, 'that there be a great darts player in these parts called one Robin Hood. Be there anyone of that name in this here tavern?'

'Aye!' saith back Robin. 'I am he. And who might you be?'

'I am the Wonderful Wozzo,' saith the stranger, 'and I can do wonders with my arrows. [*Note:* darts players call their darts 'arrows', for some reason.] 'In fact,' continueth Wozzo the Stranger, 'there is no man nor woman alive that can do the wonderful things that I can do with an arrow.'

At this all eyes in the Old Duck and Ferret turned to Robin Hood to see what he would say to this challenge. Robin gave a confident smirk.

'To that I saith,' he saith, 'duck poo. For anything thou canst do with an arrow, I can do also.'

'Verily,' saith the Stranger Wozzo, 'then I challenge thee. Dost thou accepteth my challenge?'

'Verily,' saith Robin, 'I do.'

At which Wozzo the Stranger pulled an arrow from his quiver . . . and ate it.

Everyone in the tavern gasped, and then once more all their eyes turned back to Robin. Robin hesitated for barely a second, then he too pulled an arrow from his quiver, ate it, and dropped dead.

Thus it was that Wozzo the Stranger became the winner of the first ever Eatin' an Arrow Match (afterwards known as the Eton and Harrow Match).

Snooker

Everyone knows what snooker is — it's a cross between pool and billiards where the players bash a load of coloured balls around on a large green table. The three places that are reckoned to produce the best snooker players are Great Britain, Australia and Canada. One day an enterprising businessman decided that Earth wasn't big enough for his ambitions and that the time was ripe to introduce the sport of snooker to the planet Mars. He decided that the best way to do it would be to take the best player from Britain, Australia and Canada to Mars and give a series of exhibition games, so he signed up Herbert Wally from England, Ethel la Noir from Canada, and Bruce Bobblehat from Australia.

The Martians were baffled at first by this strange game, but after a while they began to understand it. What was upsetting for poor Herbert Wally, though, was that in every game he played he was beaten by either Ethel or Bruce. When the games were over and it was time for the three snooker players to return to Earth, Herbert decided that he couldn't leave Mars with such a bad reputation. At the farewell dinner the Martians threw for them all, he decided to set the record straight and let the Martians know that he wasn't usually beaten as badly as he had been. With this in mind, Herbert banged on the table with his snooker cue and stood up.

'Dear Martians,' he began. 'First, on behalf of we three snooker players from Earth, I would like to thank you for having us here on your planet and watching us play.'

At this all the Martians clapped politely.

'However,' continued Herbert, 'you will notice that I was beaten in every game I played here. This has never happened to me before!'

The Martians, surprised, looked at each other, and then they all grinned broadly and shouted, 'Wotto!'

Herbert smiled to himself, pleased at their obvious appreciation of his statement.

'In fact,' he continued, 'on Earth I am currently the World Snooker Champion, and I am therefore the best player on the whole planet!'

At this the Martians cheered and shouted, 'Wotto!' even louder.

Herbert grinned and smirked at the two other Earth snooker players, who looked back at him, slightly miffed.

'And,' he said, 'if it hadn't been for the fact that the tip of my cue came loose in the first frame I would have thrashed both of these two players here!'

Once more the Martians shouted 'Wotto!' and applauded as Herbert sat down.

After the dinner, as the three snooker players were walking across the airfield to their spaceship, one of the Martians suddenly grabbed hold of Herbert and pushed him to one side.

'What's the matter?' asked Herbert, surprised.

'Look,' said the Martian, and pointed to a piece of smelly stuff on the ground right in Herbert's path, 'you very nearly trod right in that wotto.'

Billiards

This sport was invented by a Canadian, Bill Yards, after whom it is called.

The purpose of the game is to see who can eat the biggest pile of mashed potatoes while singing the Canadian National Anthem. This has actually never been done. It was nearly achieved by a Pierre LeClerc at the 1948 Olympic Games, but he forgot the words of the Canadian National Anthem halfway through his second helping of mashed potatoes.

The main problem with this sport is that very few competitors can remember the tune of the Canadian National Anthem. In fact it goes like this:

Da de-da-da
De da-da-tum
Something something de dum
De dum dum da dee dee.

Motor Racing

Motor Racing is illegal. Everyone knows that the speed limit in Britain is 70mph and in America 55mph, yet time and time again cars hurtle along these big concrete tracks at speeds of up to 200mph! Why are they allowed to get away with it, that's what I want to know. And when these speeding drivers stop, instead of being arrested and thrown in a deep dungeon for years, they get given bouquets of flowers and bottles of champagne!

What I can't understand is why the police aren't doing their job properly. Why aren't they waiting at the big concrete tracks to arrest these people, or chasing after them in cars with flashing blue lights? I have attempted to do my duty as a law-abiding citizen and place some of these law-breakers under Citizen's Arrest, the only trouble being that whenever I have rushed out on to these great wide concrete roads and ordered them to stop, they have run me over.

Speedway

For Speedway see my comments on motor racing. People are breaking the law by going too fast, and it ought to be stopped. The only difference between Speedway and Motor racing (apart from the fact that one is carried out in cars and one on motor bikes, but for the moment I can't remember which is which) is that in Speedway racing (yes, that's the one on motorbikes!) they use one of their feet as a brake. In fact, the championship speedway stars do special exercises every day to strengthen their brake foot, so they all have one foot bigger than the other. This has given rise to the legend of Bigfoot. Bigfoot is in fact a Speedway Rider walking to and from each race, with his brake foot in a Size 27 boot.

The saddest case I ever heard of in horse racing concerned a horse called Haggis and his jockey called Fred. Haggis and Fred had never won a race. Even worse, they had always finished last in every race they had entered. Finally the horse's owner, a woman called Dame Teresa Green, had had enough. As Fred was about to ride Haggis on to the course for a race, Dame Teresa stopped them.

'Listen,' she said to Fred, 'I am fed up. You and this terrible horse have cost me a fortune. If you don't win this race, then that's it. From tomorrow you can find another job.'

'But what about Haggis?' asked Fred.

'Him?' snorted Dame Teresa. 'If he doesn't win then I've arranged to sell him today to an old-fashioned milkman and he can spend the rest of his life pulling a milk cart.'

Poor Fred was so upset by this that he was determined that they would win. The race started, and straight away Fred started shouting in Haggis's ear, urging the horse to gallop faster. It worked for a bit, but unfortunately Haggis soon started to fall behind. In desperation Fred did a thing he had sworn he would never do, he started to hit Haggis with his whip, desperate to make the horse go faster.

'Faster!' he screamed. 'Faster!'

Instead Haggis slowed down, and finally stopped altogether.

'What's the matter?' yelled Fred. *'Why have you stopped?'*

Haggis snorted.

'It's all right for you up there,' he said. 'But don't forget, I've got to get up early tomorrow for a milk round.'

Martial Arts

Martial Arts means hitting other people with objects such as your feet or your head. It was invented by a sheriff in the American Wild West called Marshal Arts.

Martial Arts comes in many different varieties. These include judo, ju-jitsu and karate (in all of which the main object is to break a brick in half with your bare head), and origami, which involves folding up a piece of paper and poking someone with it.

The most important thing to know about Martial Arts competitions is that you need to learn to shout, 'AAIEEEE BONSAIII!!!!' very loudly, while waving your arms and legs around like a windmill. You then stop, pick up the nearest blunt instrument and bash your opponent with it.

Croquet

Croquet is a sport that was brought over from America by the famous Wild Westerner, Davy Croquet. It consists of attempting to fry a piece of fish or meat (called a Croquette) in the nude without getting injured. I have only played this once, and I did it successfully. My opponents, however, claimed that I had cheated as I was wearing clothes. I pointed out that the rules did not say that the *player* had to be in the nude, and as the piece of fish I was frying was nude then I was within the rules. Unfortunately the judges were all biased against me and they threw me out on to the street. Because of that injustice I have boycotted this game ever since, and would advise you to do the same.

Boxing

The greatest boxer of all time was Ted Fitzherbert of Ceylon. He could put anything inside a cardboard box in twenty seconds, whatever the object was. I once saw him box an elephant, a Centurion tank and a life-size model of the Eiffel Tower in twenty seconds!

After seeing him perform this astounding feat I wrote an article in a newspaper saying that Ted Fitzherbert was the greatest boxer who had ever lived. As a result of my article he got an invitation from a man called Iron Fist Lewis to challenge him for this title.

I duly escorted Ted to the competition to decide who the best boxer was. Unfortunately on the way to the meeting we lost our way and ended up in a large ring with ropes round it, where a man wearing shorts and big gloves on his fists came up to Ted, smacked him in the mouth and knocked him unconscious. I have yet to find out the name of this vandal and hooligan, but when I do I shall write to him and tell him off in no uncertain terms.

Canoeing

Among the best canoeists in the world are the Eskimos of Alaska. The kind of canoe they use is called a kayak, which is long and thin so it can get through all the frozen rivers.

Long ago, not long after the kayak had first been invented, an Eskimo called Smith was worried that if he left his kayak outside his igloo at night it would freeze solid and break in half. This had happened to a pair of trousers that he'd hung out to dry the previous night. So Smith decided that, to protect his kayak, he would take it inside his igloo with him at night and leave it by the fire to keep warm.

The next morning when he woke up, instead of his kayak being preserved by being close to the fire, it had burnt, and all that poor Smith was left with was a pile of ashes.

It was this event that gave rise to the famous Eskimo proverb, 'You can't have your kayak and heat it too,' later translated (wrongly) into English as 'You can't have your cake and eat it too.'

Wrestling

Wrestling is a really dangerous sport full of holds in which your opponent ties your body up into knots called the Half-Wellington and the Full Omelette. My cousin Percy Peabody, the family idiot, once accepted a challenge to enter a wrestling tournament against the Toughest Wrestler in Britain, a huge mountain of a man called Crusher Henshaw.

All our family turned up to watch this match, most of us wondering why on earth Percy had gone in for this contest since it was plain to see that he was only a seven stone weakling with a body like a clothes rack and muscles like string, while Crusher Henshaw had a body with muscles in places where most of us haven't even got places, and he was also known to eat herds of cattle raw with his bare teeth. However, as I said, Percy was the family idiot, so I suppose that's reason enough.

Come the day of the contest and Percy bounced into the ring looking as if the slightest puff of wind would blow him away, while Crusher crunched into the ring with a thud that made the whole hall vibrate. The bell went, and the contest got under way. Immediately Crusher grabbed Percy and proceeded to tie his windpipe into two or three intricate knots.

By the time the bell went for the end of the second round it was pretty obvious to everyone in the hall that Percy hadn't got a chance. The amazing thing was that he had managed to stay alive for so long, but everyone put that down to Crusher's good nature, despite the fact that he had spent most of the match tying and untying Percy, and jumping on him from a great height.

Just before the bell went for the beginning of the third and final round I crept over to Percy's corner, where he was lying in a reef knot on the canvas.

'Come on, Percy, give up now,' I advised, 'before he does any more damage to you!'

'No,' gasped Percy. 'It's a matter of family honour. He said that my mum's cooking was terrible.'

So that was the reason why Percy had accepted the challenge.

'Your mother's cooking *is* terrible,' I pointed out.

'Yes, I know,' he said, 'and we're allowed to say that because we're family. But Crusher Henshaw isn't family, and I'm going to make him eat his words!'

With that the bell went and Percy bounced across the ring in his reef knot. Crusher Henshaw immediately fell on him, and the next second the two of them were tied up in a knot. I closed my eyes unable to look.

From the ring I heard the sound of a yell, followed by a strangled cry, and then a huge cheer from the crowd. Fearing the worst I opened my eyes, but instead of Percy being spread in bits all over the ring, he was standing up with the referee holding his arm above his head, and Crusher Henshaw was stretched out cold on the canvas. Percy had won!

Afterwards, in the dressing room, as I helped Percy untie his knees, I asked him about what had happened in those last few seconds that had so drastically changed the outcome of the contest.

'It was amazing,' he said. 'There we were, all tied up in a complete bundle of knots, me and Crusher Henshaw, and I thought I had definitely lost. I could feel myself losing consciousness. Then suddenly you'll never believe what I saw in front of me. I saw this elbow. The opportunity was too good to miss. My hands and feet were both tied up so tightly, there was only one thing left for me to do. I leant forward, and bit the elbow as hard as I could.'

'You bit Crusher Henshaw's elbow?' I asked, shocked. 'So it was the pain that knocked him cold!'

Percy shook his head.

'No,' he said. 'Accidentally I'd bitten my own elbow. The agony was so great that I leapt out of the knot, hurtled up in the air, and hit Crusher under the chin with my head. There's nothing like biting your own elbow to give you added strength.'

Weightlifting

This sport got its name because it combines lifting heavy objects while cracking Weighter jokes. Examples of these are:

'Weighter, there's a fly in my soup.'
'Don't worry, sir, the spider on the bread will get it.'

'Weighter, do I have to sit here until I die of starvation?'
'No, madam, we close at seven.'

'Weighter, what's this in my stew?'
'I don't know, sir, all these insects look alike to me.'

'Weighter, there's a dead fly in my soup.'
'Yes, madam, they're not very good swimmers.'

Fencing

(Fencing, as everyone knows, is about nailing bits of wood to a post and sticking them down one side of your garden to stop your neighbour looking over, or their cat from coming in and walking all over your flowers, so I really don't think we can call this a sport at all. Frankly, I think that once again Ms Beaver has given me the wrong list and when she arrives at the shop to order a new fence for her garden she's going to forget what she went in there for.)

PART FOUR

Water Sports

The thing that makes Water Sports different from all other sports is that they are played in or on water. However, in England, Scotland, Ireland and Wales where it rains most of the time, all sports are played in or on water (e.g. football, tennis, cricket) and so most British sports can be called Water Sports. In Great Britain therefore the difference is as follows:

Water Sports – Sports Played Outdoors
Non-Water Sports – Sports Played Indoors

This rule is liable to change in the case of flooding due to rain or burst water pipes.

Swimming

Swimming is easy if you have webbed hands and feet. If you haven't it is quite difficult.

In my own particular experience it is easier to swim in the Shallow End than it is in the Deep End, because in the shallow end you can put your foot down every two strokes, whereas in the deep end you sink.

I would also like to point out that this is one of the drawbacks of swimming in the sea. When the tide is in the whole of the sea is Deep End, except for one little bit of Shallow End where the sand is, and the Shallow End of the sea is nearly always full of seaweed and jellyfish.

Diving

Diving means jumping off a plank into a pond of wet stuff, preferably water. However, variations are common in certain countries, e.g.:

Britain: jelly (usually raspberry or strawberry)
Australia: lager with corks in it
USA: tomato ketchup
Scandinavia: ice cream
Spain, Italy and Germany: rice pudding

Another variation, especially in hot countries where water is in short supply, is diving into a wet sponge. The most famous wet sponge diver of all was Juan de la Perez Alimento from Chile (a hot country with a cold name). Juan's career came to an abrupt and unhappy end while he was undertaking a dive from a record 2000 feet. His jealous rival, Luis Santiago, took the ultimate revenge on Juan for his magnificence: he wrung out the sponge!

Water Ski-Ing

This sport has never achieved the success its inventors hoped for, and the reason for that is because no one has yet found a lake that slopes.

Windsurfing

The greatest windsurfer in the whole Universe (with the exception of the planet Pluto) is Mark Kasporwicz, a radio presenter from Oxford in England. I know this to be a fact because he told me so.

Mark is not only the greatest windsurfer of all time but there are no distances he will not travel to find new winds to sail over (or new sails to break wind in). It was one fateful day in summer 1986 that Mark set off on his most adventurous voyage ever, to sail round the world on a solid concrete sailboard! On his first day out, he experienced major teething problems off Land's End in Cornwall, mainly because the builders had forgotten to reinforce the concrete. Without reinforcement, Mark found himself standing on one square centimetre of fast dissolving concrete, bravely holding on to the large sail. He held this pose for an amazing 0.45 of a second, then he sank.

For his second attempt he made sure that they didn't make the same mistake again.

'Don't forget to reinforce the concrete this time!' he instructed the sailboard builders firmly. And they followed his instructions faithfully. Unfortunately for Mark they used so much iron in the reinforcements that, as he launched his sailboard once more from Land's End, it sank at once.

For his third attempt Mark took no chances. This time he tied huge rockets to the back of the sailboard. His theory was that the rockets would hurl the concrete sailboard across the water from Land's End like a pebble being bounced across the ocean. Once it was well on its way the rockets would burn out and fall away, and he would continue on his journey round the world.

The Big Day arrived (for the third time). Thousands of well-wishers gathered at Land's End held their breaths in suspense and excitement as Mark's technical assistant lit the rockets at the rear of the concrete sailboard. Unfortunately for Mark the weight of the rockets pulled the back of the board down, so that when the rockets actually went off, instead of Mark's concrete sailboard hurtling across the sea, it went straight up into the air.

Right across the Universe it went, with Mark grimly hanging on to the sail, until it neared the edge of the Known Universe, and the planet Pluto. (See, I bet you were wondering where the planet Pluto came in!) At this point the rockets burnt out, and Mark's concrete sailboard plunged Pluto-wards. Down and down it went, through Pluto's atmosphere. It skidded across the planet's surface until it hit Pluto's one and only sea with a resounding Splash! And straight away it sank.

'Ah well,' said Mark, 'back to the drawing board.'

Yachting

Yachting is something that I am an expert at because I have yachted for years. The first requirement is to fill the bath with water and then put your yacht (available at most good toy shops) into it. A variation is to fill a basin with water and put your yacht in that, but personally I feel that this does not allow your yacht much room to manoeuvre. Also the soap has a tendency to slip off the bit between the taps, fall on the yacht and sink it.

Surfing

Surfing is similar to windsailing except that you don't have a sail. All that you have is a big flat ironing board which you sit on, on top of the sea, near the shore. You then wait for a huge wave to come rushing in. When it does you stand up on your ironing board, and the wave then smacks you over the head and knocks you into the water, where you get bitten by a passing shark. Altogether a Dangerous Sport.

Rowing

Rowing is what happens when adults have an argument, so it is doubtful if this can really be called a sport at all. What happens is that one adult says something, the other adult contradicts it, the first adult says, 'Don't be such an idiot!' Then they both start shouting at each other. This is called 'having a row'.

Many sports commentators confuse this activity with the one where you sit in a boat with a pair of oars and move the boat across the water with them. This is not called 'rowing' at all but is spelt and pronounced 'roeing'. Roeing is so called because sometimes fish get knocked on the head by the oars as the boat goes across the water, and throw their roe at the person in the boat in annoyance.

Water Polo

Water Polo is much the same as Polo except it is played in the water and the riders therefore ride on sea-horses.

As with Polo, this game was invented by Mark O'Polo, the famous explorer and mouth-organ player. In fact it was invented by him while he was in the bath, hence its name.

What happened was this: Mark got into the bath at the wrong end and sat down on the bath plug. He leapt out of the bath, yelling 'Eureka!' and ran out into the street where he had An Idea. The local police took one look at him, also had An Idea, and arrested him for streaking. While he was being marched off to the local police station Mark had time to invent Water Polo, the umbrella, and Archie Meedy's Principle.

As with polo, Water Polo is played with a round flat white ball with a hole in the middle.

Snorkelling

Snorkelling is really odd because you poke a length of plastic pipe up your nose, put on a glass mask, and then walk around scaring the life out of people who think you look like a Monster from Another Planet. Not really a sport at all.

It is also used as a very unfair way of going fishing, because when people walk around underwater dressed like this it scares the fish and they all faint from shock.

PART FIVE

Spectator Sports

A Spectator Sport is one where the object is to watch other people doing things. Although this may be thought to be true of most sports, Spectator Sports are different because the people being watched usually end up losing their tempers and shouting 'Go away!' or 'Who do you think you're looking at!' at the Spectator.

If they do this it means that you (the Spectator) have won the game and you can give yourself a point and a prize (e.g. an ice cream).

Watching Men Digging a Hole in the Road

This is the most widely practised spectator sport of all. In fact it is so widely practised that there really isn't a lot of fun in it any more. What has happened is that the people being looked at (i.e. the men digging the hole) have got so used to being spectated at that they now spend most of their time leaning on their shovels and pneumatic drills with their arms folded, looking at the Spectators. In other words this match is a Draw before it even begins, so frankly it is not worth bothering with.

Watching a Person who has locked Him/Herself out of His/Her House trying to get in

This is a lot of fun. You can spot the competitor (the person trying to get back in) because he/she will be running around in front of his/her house flapping his/her arms up and down. (Right, I'm giving up this his/her stuff. Let's pretend it's a man.) He will also be running from door to window and back again, tugging at the wooden edges with his finger nails.

Stand by his front gate and watch him. After a while he will notice you. If he doesn't, give a cough. When he looks at you, smile at him but say nothing. My own personal best time for this event is 2 minutes 45 seconds before the person trying to get back in started throwing things at me (his shoes).

Watching a Person whose Car has broken down

This event is easy to find. Just look in any street or country lane and sooner or later you will find a car with its bonnet up and a man or woman standing in front of it looking into the engine and scratching his/her (oh, no here we go again) head. This is the early stage of this event, so you can happily go off and do something more interesting for ten minutes or so. When you return the event will have started in earnest. By then the person will either be (a) under the car; (b) inside the engine; or (c) standing where they (right, this time it's 'they') were before but with bits of wire and mechanical objects in their hands. They will also be covered in grease and oil. It is at this stage that you begin your part in the event.

Stand near enough to them so that they notice you, but not near enough so that they can hit you with a bit of the car. As with all Spectator Sports, if they don't notice you after a few minutes, give a little cough. When they look at you, smile. When they look at you a second time in the hope that you have gone away, say, 'Having trouble with the car?'

At this point they may attempt to attack you, in which case you have won. If they decide instead to ignore you then you can dare to move a little closer. Peer over their shoulder. (Only do this if they are looking into the engine. If they are under the car, you would have to lie underneath them to look over their shoulder, which would put you in a very vulnerable position.) Say, 'Looks like the carburettor (or manifold, or starter motor).' At this point they will either tell you to go away (in which case you will have won), or they will ask your advice.

If they ask your advice then it means they know nothing about the workings of a car. If this is the case then suggest that they remove various bits of the engine. Point at these bits. Suggest that they take out some of the millions of different coloured bits of wire. When these are all lying all over the pavement, say, 'Of course, I know nothing about cars.'

(*Note:* it is advisable to say this while moving away from the person, as it is virtually certain that when you say these words they will attack you.)

Watching Someone who has got Hiccups

Watch out for someone who has got hiccups. A public place (like a bus or a train where they cannot escape) is best for this. As soon as they hiccup, stare at them. They will become so embarrassed that they will try every known way to stop hiccuping, including holding their breath. Because they are being watched they will hold their breath until their hair turns green. Keep watching them. Eventually they will either fall over unconscious, or will breathe out with a bigger hiccup than before. Either way, you will have won and can award yourself Five Points.

If they actually get up and chase you off the bus (or train), then you can give yourself another Five Points as a bonus.

Watching People Eat

This is similar to watching people with hiccups. In fact, if you do it properly, you can make the people who are eating get hiccups, and thus get yourself loads of points!

For the best fun look out for people eating spaghetti, or people trying to eat with chopsticks in a Chinese restaurant. Once they realize that you are watching them closely they will soon start making a mess. The spaghetti will start spraying the Bolognese sauce all over the restaurant with every suck. The chopsticks will cross in mid-air depositing piles of rice and messy gobs of sauce all over the table. Victory is yours when they call for a spoon.

Watching People having an Argument

Because there are two competitors in this event you can award yourself double the points if you win. However, a word of warning, this is the most dangerous Spectator Sport of all as, when their tempers finally crack, there is a very good chance that they will both unite and turn on you.

The best arguments of all to watch are those where the two people are trying to have a Private Argument (i.e. they don't want anyone else to know). When you find an argument like this going on, stick to the two competitors like glue. While they know they are being watched they will clam up and pretend to be friendly, and wait for you to go away. Stay with them. Soon the tension of wanting to continue their argument will prove too much for them and they will yell at you things like, 'Well?' and, 'Who are you looking at?' Say, 'Oh, I'm sorry, I didn't see you two there,' and carry on looking at them.

It is when they offer to punch you on the nose that you know that you have won. Do not test the seriousness of this offer; they will not be bluffing.

Afterduction

I bet you're wondering what an Afterduction is. Well, an *Intro*duction comes at the start of the book and lets you know that the book is about to begin, so an *After*duction is the thing that comes at the end of the book and lets you know it's finished.

This may sound pretty obvious to you, but I am told by Ms Beaver that it is not obvious to some people. Some people are so dim that they don't realize a book has finished just because they've finished reading the last page. These people turn the last page over, find they're at the front of the book and start reading it all over again.

People like these are idiots! I know because my Uncle Percy was such an idiot. He once spent ten years reading the same mystery book over and over again because he didn't realize it had ended. My Aunt Penelope once asked him, 'But didn't you notice that the Detective said that it was the butler who had done the robbery at the end of the book?'

'I did notice,' said Uncle Percy, 'but I just thought he kept getting away and carried on stealing more jewels. Although I did wonder why he kept stealing the same lot of jewels over and over again.'

So, for my Uncle Percy and all other idiots like him, that was . . .

THE AFTERDUCTION

JOKE BOOKS

Have you heard about all the hilarious joke books published by Beaver? They are available in bookshops or they can be ordered directly from us. Just complete the form below and enclose the right amount of money and the books will be sent to you at home.

☐	THE SMELLY SOCKS JOKE BOOK	Susan Abbott	£1.95
☐	THE VAMPIRE JOKE BOOK	Peter Eldin	£1.50
☐	THE WOBBLY JELLY JOKE BOOK	Jim Eldridge	£1.50
☐	A JUMBLE OF JUNGLY JOKES	John Hegarty	£1.50
☐	NOT THE ELEPHANT JOKE BOOK	John Hegarty	£1.50
☐	THE CRAZY CRAZY JOKE BAG	Janet Rogers	£1.95
☐	THE CRAZIEST JOKE BOOK EVER	Janet Rogers	£1.50
☐	THE ELEPHANT JOKE BOOK	Katie Wales	£1.00
☐	THE RETURN OF THE ELEPHANT JOKE BOOK	Katie Wales	£1.50
☐	JOKES FROM OUTER SPACE	Katie Wales	£1.25
☐	SANTA'S CHRISTMAS JOKE BOOK	Katie Wales	£1.50

If you would like to order books, please send this form, and the money due to:
ARROW BOOKS, BOOKSERVICE BY POST, PO BOX 29, DOUGLAS, ISLE OF MAN, BRITISH ISLES. Please enclose a cheque or postal order made out to Arrow Books Ltd for the amount due including 22p per book for postage and packing both for orders within the UK and for overseas orders.

NAME ....

ADDRESS ....

....

Please print clearly.

Whilst every effort is made to keep prices low it is sometimes necessary to increase cover prices at short notice. Arrow Books reserve the right to show new retail prices on covers which may differ from those previously advertised in the text or elsewhere.